CURIOUS PEARL

SCIENCE GIRL

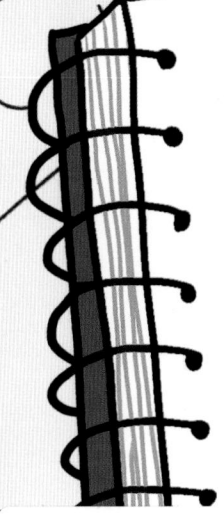

CURIOUS PEARL KICKS OFF FORCES AND MOTION

by Eric Braun

illustrated by Anthony Lewis

raintree

one company — publishers for children

Curious Pearl here!
Do you like science?

I certainly do! I have all sorts of fun tools to help me observe and investigate, but my favourite tool is my science notebook. That's where I write down questions and facts that help me learn more about science. Would you like to join me on my science adventures? You're in for a special surprise!

It's Sunday – and that means football! I play on the Rainbow Dragons with my friends Sabina and Sal. Today is our last match of the season. While I waited for my friends, I decided to rearrange the pumpkins on our front steps. Autumn is a beautiful season, don't you think?

Except, the big pumpkin was too heavy for me to lift. And the little one kept rolling down the steps as if it had a mind of its own. Ugh!

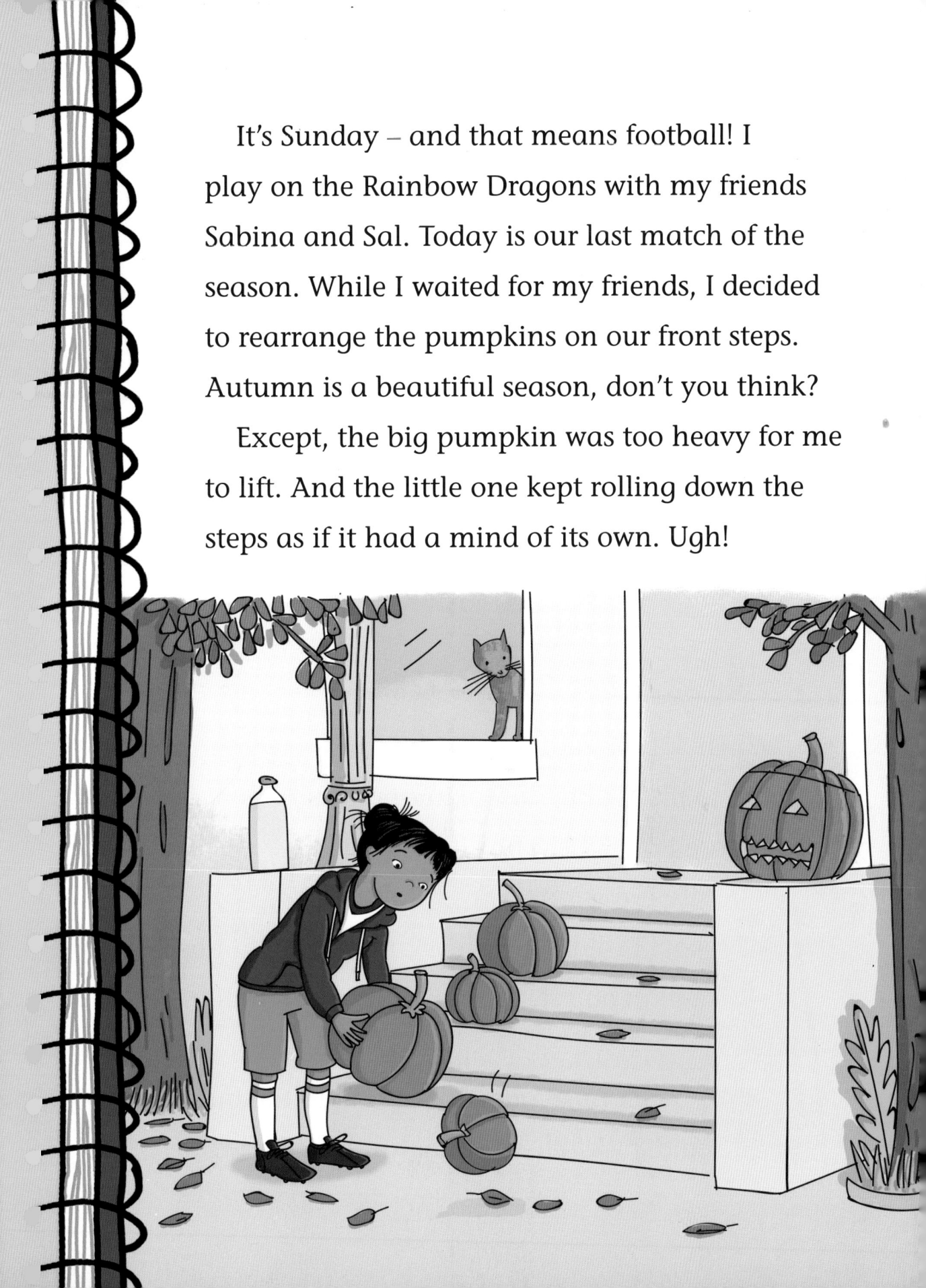

When Sabina and Sal arrived, they saw me
trying to lift the big pumpkin and laughed.
I suppose I did look a bit silly.

"Gravity is a strong force," Sal said.

"Eureka!" I said. "A force is anything that pushes
or pulls on an object. Gravity pulls everything
down."

"We'd better push ourselves along to the match,"
Sabina said. "We'll help you with this afterwards."

While we warmed up for the match, I kept thinking about those pumpkins. How could I get the big one to the top step?

Sal kicked a ball up into the air, and I thought about all the different types of pushes and pulls there are. Gravity, kicks, wind . . . even if the air is still, it is pushing on us. Forces can have different strengths and directions.

Finally it was time to start the match. Our
opponents, the Funky All-Stars, got to kick-off. Sabina
intercepted one of their passes. The ball was coming
at her fast, but she stopped it with her foot.

"Eureka!" I shouted to her. "Your foot was a force
on that ball. A force can create motion – or stop it."

"What?" she asked. She started dribbling towards
the goal, but then she looked back. She was surprised
at what she saw. "Are you writing in your notebook?"

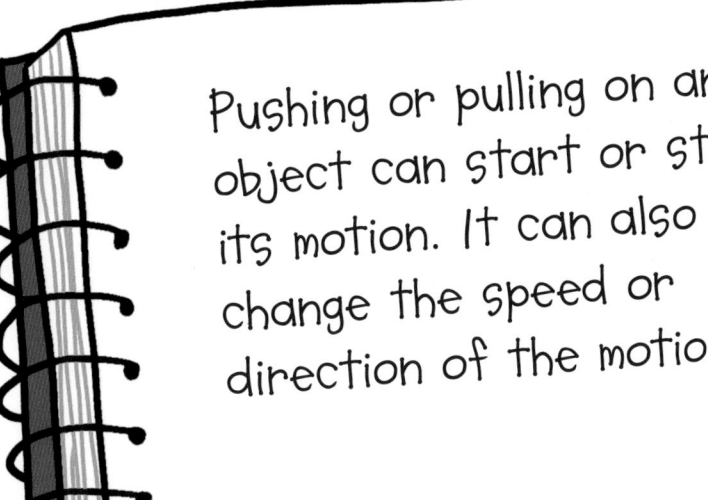

"Well, yes," I said. "This is important."

I never go anywhere without my trusty science notebook! I jotted down what I'd noticed.

Pushing or pulling on an object can start or stop its motion. It can also change the speed or direction of the motion.

A defender tried to take the ball away from Sabina, so she passed it to Sal. It went straight to him.

"Nice pass!" I yelled.

Sal closed in on the goal and kicked the ball hard. Bang! The goalie caught it.

"Good try, Sal!" I said. "You put more force on the ball, making it go faster. A bigger push or pull makes things move more quickly.

A softer force makes things move more slowly."

"Great!" Sal said. "But watch out – the goalie is kicking the ball your way!"

"I'm ready," I said.

The goalie kicked the ball really far! It went past me, and I didn't get to it. What could I have done differently?

At half-time, Coach Lindsay had some advice. "Don't go where the ball is. Go to where it will be! That way you can intercept it," she said.

"Coach?" I asked. "How do you know where the ball will be?"

Coach Lindsay said, "If you watch what the ball has been doing, you can usually predict what it will do next. First you observe, then you predict."

Now Coach was talking my language – science language. I made a note in my notebook.

The patterns of an object's motion can be observed and measured. When past motion shows a regular pattern, future motion can be predicted from it.

We started warming up for the second half. I watched as the balls flew through the air, then rolled on the ground, then stopped. I remembered how Sabina stopped a ball with her foot during the game. But what made the ball stop?

Lucky for me, my football coach is also my science teacher! She knows practically everything there is to know about science. So I asked her what makes a ball stop when there's no force stopping it.

"But there IS a force stopping it," Coach said. "It's called friction. Friction happens when two objects rub against each other. The ground and the air are putting friction on the ball."

"I think I understand!" I said. I made a note in my science notebook.

Friction is a force that slows down objects. It also causes heat. That's why we rub our hands together when we are cold!

Sal, Sabina and I kicked a few more balls around. I kicked some hard and high. I kicked some softly. I kicked some straight and some sideways. My foot put a different amount of force on the ball every time.

Then I kicked one and it crashed into Sal's ball. They both rolled away in different directions.

"Hey!" Sal joked. "Leave my ball alone."

"Sorry!" I said. "But – eureka!"

"What have you discovered this time?" Sal asked.

"The force from my foot can push on the ball I kick. But it can push on another ball, too."

"Guys!" Sabina called. "Time to get back on the pitch."

I made a quick note in my science notebook.

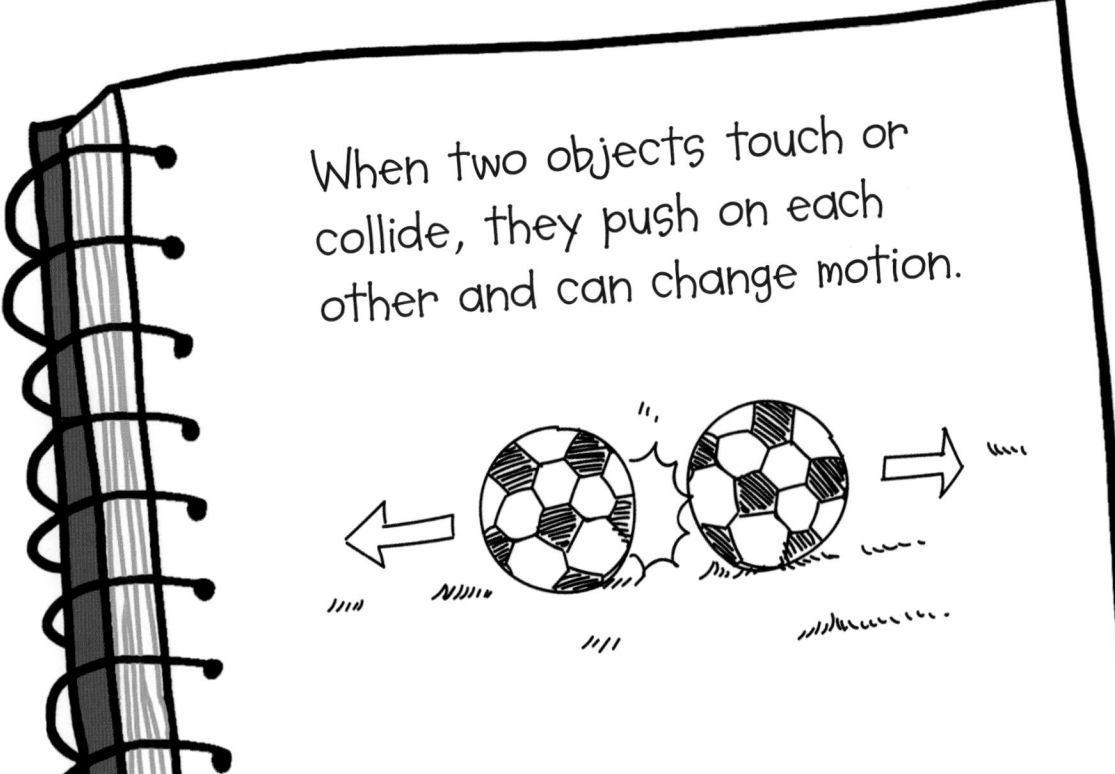

When two objects touch or collide, they push on each other and can change motion.

The ref blew the whistle to start the second half. I got to take the kick-off. As I looked at the ball, I thought about the forces that were acting on that ball. Gravity was pulling it down. Air was pushing in all around it. But the ball wasn't moving. Before I kicked, I made a quick note in my notebook.

An object at rest will stay at rest unless a force acts on it. This is called inertia.

Then I kicked the ball. That kick was the biggest force of all!

Sabina and another player got to the ball at the same time. The ball was trapped between their feet. Both of them were kicking the ball, but it wasn't moving much. When two forces work in opposite directions, they can cancel each other out.

Late in the match, the ball rolled my way. I trapped it with my foot, stopping its motion. Then I dribbled the ball between my feet to keep the ball in motion. When I got close enough to the goal, I blasted the ball towards the net.

GOAL!

"Eureka!" yelled Sabina and Sal. One point for
the Rainbow Dragons!

After the match, Sabina brought up the issue of the big pumpkin again. She said, "We can solve this pumpkin problem using what we know about forces and motion."

"You're right," I said. "I think the solution is simple. We need a stronger force pulling up on the pumpkin."

"How do we get that?" Sabina asked.

Sal had an idea. "Teamwork!"

Now, that's our kind of force!

Balloon race

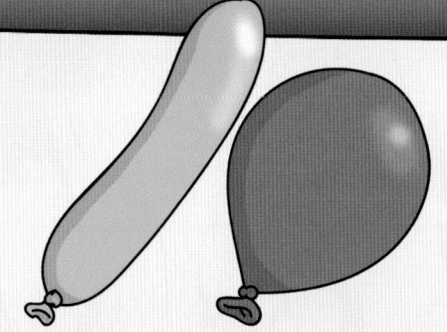

Try this balloon-racing experiment to compare
the friction on different-sized objects.

Here's what you need

- 4-metre length
  of string
- 1 straw
- Tape

- 2 or more balloons of
  different sizes (it's helpful
  to have a big round one
  and a long narrow one)
- Optional: a stopwatch
  to time results

Steps:

1. Slip the straw onto the string. Tie one end of the string
   to a doorknob. Tie or tape the other end to something on
   the opposite end of the room.

2. Blow up one of the balloons and hold it shut (don't tie it).

3. Slide the straw all the way to one end of the string. Tape
   the top of the balloon onto the straw so the opening faces
   the end of the string.

4. Let go of the opening. Time how long it takes to shoot
   down the string to the other end.

The air shooting out of the balloon creates a force
that pushes it forwards. The air surrounding the balloon
slows it. Experiment with your different-sized balloons.
Why do you think some go faster or further?

21

GLOSSARY

force push or pull that can change the motion of an object

friction resistance a moving object encounters from other objects

gravity natural force that pulls objects towards the ground

inertia resistance of any object to change its state of motion (speed or direction)

motion when an object changes its position over time

observe watch something closely

predict work out what will happen in the future based on what you have observed in the past

READ MORE

Forces and Motion (Essential Physical Science), Angela Royston (Raintree, 2014)

Science Encyclopedia, Kirsteen Robson (Usborne Publishing, 2015)

When Forces and Motion Collide (Engage Literacy), Chris Oxlade (Raintree, 2017)

WEBSITES

www.bbc.com/education/topics/zvpp34j
Learn more about pushes and pulls!

www.dkfindout.com/uk/science/forces-and-motion
Find out more about forces and motion.

COMPREHENSION ACTIVITIES

Describe the different forces and motion that occur in your favourite sport and how they can be influenced.

Experiment with letting a toy car roll down an inclined board. Add weight to the car by taping a penny or something else to the top. Change the texture of the board by wrapping it in cloth, paper and sandpaper. Explain why the speed and distance of the car change.

BOOKS IN THIS SERIES

INDEX

Thanks to our advisor for his expertise, research and advice:
Paul Ohmann, PhD.

Raintree is an imprint of Capstone Global Library Limited,
a company incorporated in England and Wales having its
registered office at 264 Banbury Road, Oxford, OX2 7DY
Registered company number: 6695582

www.raintree.co.uk
myorders@raintree.co.uk

Text © Capstone Global Library Limited 2019
The moral rights of the proprietor have been asserted.

Designed by Ted Williams and Nathan Gassman
Cover illustrated by Stephanie Dehennin
The illustrations in the book were digitally produced.
Original illustrations © Capstone Global Library Limited 2019
Production by Tori Abraham
Originated by Capstone Global Library Ltd
Printed and bound in India

ISBN 978 1 4747 6321 9
22 21 20 19 18
10 9 8 7 6 5 4 3 2 1

British Library Cataloguing in Publication Data
A full catalogue record for this book is available from the British
Library.

Every effort has been made to contact copyright holders of
material reproduced in this book. Any omissions will be rectified
in subsequent printings if notice is given to the publisher.

All the internet addresses (URLs) given in this book were valid at
the time of going to press. However, due to the dynamic nature
of the internet, some addresses may have changed, or sites may
have changed or ceased to exist since publication. While the
author and publisher regret any inconvenience this may cause
readers, no responsibility for any such changes can be accepted
by either the author or the publisher.